A Simple Guide to Self Awareness

Using the Myers-Briggs Typology and CG Jung's theory

The purpose of life is to align with the soul's blueprint which is to be found by going within. Life is like a treasure hunt where each clue brings the personality closer to this blueprint. The hunt begins with knowledge of, and respect for, ourself and our travelling companions and extends to an appreciation that we are merely a cell in the Cosmic energy body.

This book invites the reader to begin the inward journey.

Joy Nugent other books:

As Good as Goodbyes Get – a window into death and dying, 2014
My Way – one nurse's passion for end-of-life, 2018
Parting the Veil – reflections on soul, 2018.
Your Life – Your Way – practical tips and reflections, 2022.
Live Well to Die Well - looking at all facets of a best possible life, 2023.
A Self-Care Portfolio, 2023

A Simple Guide to Self Awareness
Copyright © 2023 Joy Nugent

Inquiries and Book Orders should be addressed to:

www.soultalksbooks.com

Email: joy.nugent@internode.on.net
Phone: (213) 814-3974
Address: 500 Terry Francois Street San Francisco, CA 94158

Contents

The journey to self-awareness requires guidelines to be followed. These are basic guidelines for the use of the MBTI:

- Understanding type preferences begins the process of self-discovery in order to have an appreciation of the preferences of others and ourselves.

- There is a wide range of behaviour within each type and stereotyping is to be avoided. Human beings are both unique and complex.

- It is important to remember that type indicates preferences not behaviour—people will use behaviours not based on their preferences to adapt to unusual situations or when survival is threatened.

- MBTI does not measure ability.

- It is a starting point for discussion and appreciating differences. Type is dynamic; we continue to develop our type and learn to appreciate and to express the ever-changing facets of our personality. We are work in progress towards knowledge of the whole Self. The Self refers to those parts of us that are conscious, unconscious, and also part of the collective unconscious.

MBTI as a mentor

A mentor acts like a mirror to a person receiving the mentoring or guidance. The 'mirror' (mentor) helps a person to see themselves more clearly and as they really are. The MBTI is such a mentoring tool.

Everyone is Unique

At one stage or another we have all probably said that everyone is different. How much influence does the environment a person lives in shape behaviour and how much is determined at birth? The Swiss psychologist CG Jung (1969) believed that we are born with preferences and while a person may adapt to an environment, the MBTI demonstrates that there is a basic preference for what energises a person, how a person gains information, how a person processes that information and how a person lives in the world. While each individual is unique, preferences can be appreciated when we consider the hand preferred for writing.

An Overview of the Myers-Briggs Typology Index

Katherine Briggs was a woman who studied biographies and noted character differences in the 1920s. She realised that people responded to situations in different ways and how they responded was often from their basic personality. She studied the psychological types which had been described by Carl Jung (1969) and, with the help of her daughter Isabel Briggs-Myers, developed Carl Jung's research and their own findings into a typology. This is known world-wide as the **MBTI** (Myers Briggs Typology Indicator) and is used extensively for the creation of effective teamwork in business and health institutions. I believe it is useful for health professionals in understanding and building rapport and communicating with those in their care and their colleagues as well as for understanding their own uniqueness. If a person is listened to and understood, he/she feels validated and less likely to express frustrations and difficulties in unacceptable ways. This is also true for people with dementia. Having a working knowledge of the MBTI is helpful in appreciating the differences and indeed the skills of individuals.

Jung believed that people collect information about their world through their senses **(Sensing)** and through their intuition **(IN tuition)**. He believed that people make decisions about that information with either the head **(Thinking)** or the heart **(Feeling)**. He recognised that people received their energy in two different ways: from their external world **(Extroverts)** and from their internal world (Introverts). Katherine Briggs added two more distinctions. She saw that people related to their outside world by being decisive **(Judging)** and by 'going with the flow' **(Perceiving)**.

By considering **Introversion, Extroversion, Sensing, iNtuition, Thinking, Feeling, Judging** and **Perceiving**, 16 different types of people were identified. The following descriptions expand a little on the gifts and characteristics of each type. The work of this mother and daughter is intended to bring about peace and harmony in relationships through the understanding that we are all valuable and gifted—in different ways. For example:

Extrovert types prefer to relate to the outer world of people and things rather than to the inner world of ideas. They like variety and action and are often good at greeting people. They are impatient with long slow jobs and often act quickly and sometimes without thinking. They talk to think and so put their ideas outside of them for processing. Some patients are like this and they like to talk through their problems or their symptoms and will appreciate people and things around them. They may repeat a conversation so as to take in the meaning.

Introvert types prefer to relate more to the inner world of ideas than to the outer world of people and things. They like quiet for concentration, and tend to be careful with details. They tend to dislike sweeping statements and have trouble remembering names and facts. They like to work alone. They think and then talk. Patients with this characteristic will want time to think through internally the information that they have been given and may take time to decide what it is that they want. They can be quite stressed by a lot of things going on around them or a lot of people at one time.

Sensing types prefer to work with known facts than look for new possibilities and relationships. They don't like new problems unless there are standard ways to solve them—preferring an established way of doing things. They enjoy using skills already learned more than learning new ones and seldom make errors of fact. They are good at precise work and patient with routine details. It is these patients who may want details of the treatment and will be reluctant to try something that is new and not proven. They may prefer to be cared for in a known environment and have confidence in people they already know and trust. These patients appreciate continuity of care and a routine.

Intuitive types prefer to look for possibilities and relationships than known facts. They like solving new problems and dislike doing the same thing repeatedly. They enjoy learning a new skill more than using it and work in bursts of energy powered by enthusiasm with slack periods in between. They reach a conclusion quickly and are impatient with routine details. These patients are more likely to try new treatments and new environments. They may adapt more quickly to a loss of body function, eg. loss of hair, or mobility. They may have irrational ways of 'knowing' and may seem to have read a person's thoughts.

Thinking types prefer to base judgements more on impersonal analysis and logic than on personal values. They do not show emotion readily and are often uncomfortable dealing with people's feelings and may hurt people's feeling without knowing it. Health professionals need to be aware of this when an advocate situation arises. Thinking types like analysis and putting things into logical order and tend to decide impersonally without paying attention to people's wishes. They are able to reprimand people or fire them when necessary. As a patient they will need encouragement to express feelings and be reminded that expressions such as tears are healthy and natural. They may wish to be involved in their health records and in writing their biography.

Feeling types prefer to base judgement more on personal values than on impersonal analysis and logic. They tend to be very aware of other people and their feelings and enjoy pleasing people. They dislike telling people unpleasant things and tend to be sympathetic and like harmony. It is important, too, for feeling types to be involved with people for best use of their skills. However, because they like to please they may find breaking 'bad' news difficult. As carers, feeling types need to be reminded of the need and benefit of 'tough love'. As a patient they may not want to hurt the doctor or nurse by refusing treatment or fear that if they do not please, they will be rejected.

Perceiving types prefer a flexible spontaneous way of life better than a planned, decided, orderly way. They adapt well to changing situations and do not mind leaving things open for alteration and may have trouble making decisions. They may start too many projects and have difficulty in finishing them. Perceiving types, as patients, may wish to try many different types of treatments and are not so particular when changes are made to their environment or routine. It may be frustrating for their advocate to know what it is they really want.

     A SIMPLE GU IDE TO SELF - AWARENESS

Judging types prefer a planned, decided, orderly way of life better than a flexible, spontaneous way. They work best when they can plan their work and follow the plan. They like to get things settled and finished and may decide things too quickly. They may dislike interrupting the project they are working on for a more urgent one. As patients, these types will appreciate a strict regime for medication and treatment and written instructions. They may be frustrated by not being able to complete arrangements concerning their affairs—especially in situations where they suspect that information is being withheld. They may decide too quickly to cease a treatment.

Putting the MBTI into practice

Obviously as people go through life they adapt and compensate for certain characteristics. For example, if a receptionist who is an introvert and a thinking type is to be effective in their position, he/she will have to develop extrovert feeling qualities in order to make people feel welcome and to adapt to interruptions from the telephone. Having an awareness of the MBTI helps us to relate effectively to each other as team members, and to patients. With a knowledge

of our preferences, we are able to strive for balance, in our working life and in our time for relaxation.

The patterns in a person's behaviour, as indicated by the MBTI, can assist those who are planning care and accommodation placement. When it comes to making decisions, an appreciation of a person's personality is helpful. For example, a perceiving personality will have trouble being decisive while a person with a preference for judging may make decisions too quickly. An individual with a preference for thinking may make decisions concerning treatment based on logic rather than listening to the heart. The relationships between the team members are enhanced when differences are respected and valued.

Temperament

Two American psychologists, Keirsey and Bates, are known for their work on temperament theory. When considering temperament, a unique set of wants, abilities and stressors emerge as themes. Keirsey and Bates defined four temperaments:

IDEALIST
intuition & feeling NF

People with a temperament which combines intuition and feeling, are often referred to as IDEALISTS. They are interested in personal growth and improving the world. They are interested in becoming self-actualised and reaching their potential.

Questions asked

- How does this affect other's morale?
- Who needs to know?
- What impact does this have on the organisation's principles?
- What is most important to people?

They value: Autonomy, cooperation, harmony and self-determination

Irritations at work

- Impersonal treatment
- Criticism
- Lack of positive feedback

GUARDIAN
sensing & judging SJ

People with a temperament which combines sensing and judging, are often referred to as GUARDIANS. They like to feel part of an organisation and have a place in the scheme of things. They are responsible and accountable and like to serve.

Questions asked

- What is the order?
- What is my duty?
- Why change?
- How is this justified?
- Does it work?

They value: Caution, carefulness, accuracy

Irritations at work

- Others not employing standard operating procedures
- Ignored deadlines
- Others not playing by the rules

RATIONAL
intuition & thinking NT

People with a temperament that combines intuition and thinking as opposed to intuition and feeling, are referred to as RATIONALS. They like to be competent and value knowledge and the power of the intellect. They are the visionaries and may seem to have their heads in the clouds and be sceptical.

Questions asked

- What is involved?
- What is the strategy?
- Who has the power?
- What is the system?

They value: Competence, intelligence, complexity and principles

Irritations at work

- Things that are redundant
- Stupid errors
- Illogical actions
- Impatient with human concerns

ARTISAN
sensing & perceiving SP

People with a temperament that combines sensing and perceiving as opposed to sensing and judging, enjoy action, freedom and spontaneity. They are the negotiators and make instantaneous decisions from many possibilities. They are difficult to tie down and are known as ARTISANS.

Questions asked

- What is the need right now?
- What are the stakes?
- Where is the crisis?
- How soon can we go and do?

They value: Flexibility, change, taking risks, action

Irritations at work

- Restrictions
- Being told how to work
- Doing it 'the way it's always been done'
- Not being able to give immediate response

A Glossary of Jungian Terms

Conscious   That part of ourselves of which we are aware.

Ego   Ego is a person's story. It is what a person identifies themselves with—"I drive a Porcha," "I am an electrician," "I am the Mayor," "I am a single mother" etc. They may identify with their suffering and a perceived injustice.

Ego resists death and enjoys being in control. Growth and consciousness are achieved when the ego-self dies to the deeper meaning of life. This meaning is to be aware of the soul which does not die and travels from lifetime to lifetime experiencing a physical existence.

Ego is a lens through which a person views life. However, the lens may be distorted by memories, thoughts, and feelings. There are many factors that influence a person's view of life and give a sense of meaning. Understanding of these comes with self-awareness.

The Persona   The 'persona' is the organised image of 'self' formed to present to the outside world—partly conscious and partly unconscious.

It is snapshot of a consciously held belief of the person we are at this point in time.

If such a belief is one of poor self-image or disaffirming identity, the person may become depressed or contemplate suicide.

We are more than our persona!

In times of stress or grief, a person may regress to a former persona—(eg. become a dependent child).

This is merely a former state of being and not new life. A person's persona may project a superficial or inappropriate role or identity and be a false self.

True Self   True self is the joining of the conscious and unconscious. Edward Whitmont tells us that only through critical times of suffering and despair can transformation occur.

When we find our true Self we can accept that we are here for a special purpose—to fulfil our own personal myth or, in the language of CG Jung, our own personal archetype or instinctual nature (eg. Wise Old Man, the Great Mother, the Magician, the Seeker, Lover, Creative One, the god or goddess).

The Self is the centre of the person. It is the central guidance system—the God within. CG Jung believed that a person lives in order to obtain the greatest possible amount of spiritual development and self-awareness.

Jung called this lifetime work, individuation—the process of becoming whole or the process of becoming our true self and finding our own unique way.

The Shadow	It contains parts of us that are not compatible with the persona's image of ourselves.

The Shadow

It contains parts of us that are not compatible with the persona's image of ourselves.

It contains unlived lives—including potentialities.

It may contribute to 'terminal restlessness'.

It is connected to the Inferior Function (a person's least preferred way in the world).

Inferior Function

Is the least preferred of the Four Functions—consequently the weakest and least developed and operates in your least important world.

Is seen when stressed, ill, tired or under the influence of drugs.

Behaviour can become compulsive—the person is unable to stop even if conscious mind wants to.

A tremendous charge of emotions is felt when the inferior function takes control.

Often ideas, thoughts and feelings that arise are not grounded in reality.

States of inflation or hopelessness and gloom are experienced—moody. Eg. the Inferior Function of an ENFJ is introverted thinking.

Each person has their strengths and weaknesses.

The behaviour of person's Inferior Function causes the greatest suffering and stress.

Unless a high degree of awareness of one's potential weakness has been achieved, the Inferior Function remains primitive, childish and tyrannical.

Anima

The unconscious feminine, usually thought of as being in the male.

Allows for relatedness, receptivity, and emotionality.

If not integrated into consciousness, a person may feel lonely, be abstract, and swept by moods that prohibit true feeling.

It is often projected onto another rather than honoured as part of the individual's psyche.

Robert Johnson, the noted lecturer and Jungian analyst says that the feminine side of a man is to connect him within the depths of his inner being and to make a bridge to his deepest self.

Animus

The unconscious masculine—usually thought of as being in the female.

Allows for focus, discrimination and the ability to find meaning in ideas.

If not integrated into consciousness, a person may become very opinionated and unable to focus clearly.

It is often projected onto another rather than honoured as part of the individual's psyche.

Robert Johnson describes a woman's parallel to male moods as being delivered over to her inner masculine side and thus subject to a sharpness, a challenging, a needling quality which is a type of poor-quality masculinity.

The Personal Unconcious

The unconscious needs to be explored for it is wiser than we are and is our interface with God - Scott Peck, (1997)

The unconscious communicates through a symbolic language.

It may be in a dream or a feeling that is roused when we look at a cross, a country's flag, a painting or hear a particular sound like the sea or a piece of music.

It has been said that art and music are the language of the soul.

Flames may be a symbol of purification while the snake is the traditional symbol of healing. Fairy tales are full of symbolic language.

Professor Ian Maddocks says that cancer itself is a symbol—a symbol of death and decay.

Sports heroes and actors have become symbols.

Princess Diana was for many a symbol representing the struggle of life, the disappointments, betrayal, hope, service to others, caring, motherhood, beauty and humanness.

The four-wheel drive motor vehicle has become a symbol of adventure and back to nature environments.

Images are the building blocks of our personalities and influence our coping skills and ideas. An image or memory is something experienced that has gone into the unconscious. If our images are positive and self-affirming that pattern is likely to continue, but if the images are negative and self-defeating, that pattern is also likely to continue unless the cycle is broken.

What is needed to bring about health of body, mind and psyche are images that lead to new patterns of thought and different outcomes. By transforming old self-limiting images, a creative change can occur. However, these images need to be brought to awareness for this transformation to occur.

Triggers can release the memory. The Swiss psychiatrist Dr Elisabeth Kubler-Ross says that feelings are like 'pockets of pus'—they need to be released so that healing can take place. Healing takes place from the bottom.

Change

To bring about change in their lives, they have to experience despair and to face the black night of their tunnelled state of mind in order to come out into the light of change.

- Jane Wheelwright, Jungian analyst

We have many parts in the one body,
And all these parts have different functions.
In the same way, though we are many,
we are one body in union . . .
We are all joined to each other as
different parts of one body.
Having then gifts differing . . . .
- Romans. 12: 4-8

Characteristics Frequently Associated with Each Type

ISTJ Quiet, serious, earn success by thoroughness and dependability. Practical, matter-of-fact, realistic and responsible. Decide logically what should be done and work toward it steadily, regardless of distractions. Take pleasure in making everything orderly and organise—their work, their home, their life. Value traditions and loyalty.	**ISFJ** Quiet, friendly, responsible and conscientious. Committed and steady in meeting their obligations. Thorough, painstaking and accurate. Loyal, considerate, notice and remember specifics about people who are important to them, concerned with how others feel. Strive to create an orderly and harmonious environment at work and at home.
ISTP Tolerant and flexible, quiet observers until a problem appears, then act quickly to find workable solutions. Analyse what makes things work and readily get through large amounts of data to isolate the core of practical problems. Interested in cause and effect, organise facts using logical principles, value efficiency.	**ISFP** Quiet, friendly, sensitive, and kind. Enjoy the present moment, what's going on around them. Like to have their own space and to work within their own time frame. Loyal and committed to their values and to people who are important to them. Dislike disagreements and conflicts, do not force their opinions or values on others.
ESTP Flexible and tolerant, they take a pragmatic approach focused on immediate results. Theories and conceptual explanations bore them—they want to act energetically to solve the problem. Focus on the here-and-now, spontaneous, enjoy each moment that they can be active with others. Enjoy material comforts and style. Learn best through doing.	**ESFP** Outgoing, friendly and accepting. Exuberant lovers of life, people and material comforts. Enjoy working with others to make things happen. Bring common sense and a realistic approach to their work and make work fun. Flexible and spontaneous, adapt readily to new people and environments. Learn best by trying a new skill with other people.
ESTJ Practical, realistic, matter-of-fact. Decisive, quickly move to implement decisions. Organise projects and people to get things done, focus on getting results in the most efficient way possible. Take care of routine details. Have a clear set of logical standards, systematically follow them and want others to also. Forceful in implementing their plans.	**ESFJ** Warm-hearted, conscientious, and cooperative. Want harmony in their environment, work with determination to establish it. Like to work with others to complete tasks accurately and on time. Loyal, follow through even in small matters. Notice what others need in their day-to-day lives and try to provide it. Want to be appreciated for who they are and for what they contribute.

INFJ	INTJ
Seek meaning and connection in ideas, relationships and material possessions. Want to understand what motivates people and are insightful about others. Conscientious and committed to their firm values. Develop a clear vision about how best to serve the common good. Organised and decisive in implementing their vision.	Have original minds and great drive for implementing their ideas and achieving their goals. Quickly see patterns in external events and develop long-range explanatory perspectives. When committed, organise a job and carry it through. Sceptical and independent, have high standards of competence and performance—for themselves and others.
INFP	INTP
Idealistic, loyal to their values and to people who are important to them. Want an external life that is congruent with their values. Curious, quick to see possibilities, can be catalysts for implementing ideas. Seek to understand people and to help them fulfil their potential. Adaptable, flexible and accepting unless a value is threatened.	Seek to develop logical explanations for everything that interest them. Theoretical and abstract, interested more in ideas than in social interaction. Quiet, contained, flexible and adaptable. Have unusual ability to focus in depth to solve problems in their area of interest. Sceptical, sometimes critical, always analytical.
ENFP	ENTP
Warmly enthusiastic and imaginative. See life as full of possibilities. Make connections between events and information very quickly and confidently proceed based on the patterns they see. Want a lot of affirmation from others and readily give appreciation and support. Spontaneous and flexible, often rely on their ability to improvise and their verbal fluency.	Quick, ingenious, stimulating, alert and outspoken. Resourceful in solving new and challenging problems. Adept at generating conceptual possibilities and then analysing them strategically. Good at reading other people. Bored by routine, will seldom do the same thing the same way, apt to turn to one new interest after another.
ENFJ	ENTJ
Warm, empathetic, responsive, and responsible. Highly attuned to the emotions, needs and motivations of others. Find potential in everyone, want to help othrs fulfil their potential. May act as catalysts for individual and group growth. Loyal, responsive to praise and criticism. Sociable, facilitate others in a group and provide inspiring leadership.	Frank, decisive, assume leadership readily. Quickly see illogical and inefficient procedures and policies, develop and implement comprehensive systems to solve organisational problems. Enjoy long-term planning and goal setting. Usually well informed, well read, enjoy expanding their knowledge and passing it on to others. Forceful in presenting their ideas.

Using the MBTI in the process of Self Discovery

With the catch cry, "we don't know what we don't know" in mind, the following is intended to open a door just a little way so that the reader can, if they desire, pursue with an appropriate professional this therapeutic tool for self-discovery. Understanding type preference is one way to begin the process of self-discovery and will allow an appreciation of the preferences of others as well as ourselves.

There is a wide range of behaviour within each type and stereotyping is to be avoided. For example, it is not helpful to say, "What can you expect from an SJ?" It is acknowledged that behaviours are not based on preferences and people are able to adapt to unusual situations or when survival is threatened. For example, when a relationship or job demands that we perform in a certain way.

As well as considering Temperament and Psychological Type, a person will have a life-time of coping skills, personal beliefs and values which make up the rich patterns in their life. The MBTI is not about skills or ability. Finding meaning will include considering how a life is lived in the outer world and how a life is lived in the inner world. The inner world can be explored by a person considering their least preferred functions (Inferior). These are largely unconscious as the following diagram illustrates:

A review of how the different types receive energy

Extrovert (E)	Introvert (I)
external	internal
outside activity	insider pull
blurt it out	keep it in
breadth	depth
involved with people	work with ideas, thoughts
interaction	concentration
action	reflection
do-think-do	think-do-think

A review of how the different types collect information

Sensing (S)	Intuition (N)
use the five senses	sixth sense, hunches
what is real	what could be
practical	theoretical
be in the present time	future possibilities
look for facts	insights
use established skills	learning new skills
what is useful?	where is the novelty?
step-by-step approach	leap around approach

A review of how the different types process information

Thinking (T)	Feeling (F)
head	heart
logical system	value system
objective	subjective
justice	mercy
critique	compliment
principles	harmony
reason	empathy
firm but fair	compassionate

A review of how the different types live in the outside world

Judgement (J)	Perception (P)
planful	spontaneous
regulate	flow
control	adapt
settled	tentative
run one's life	let life happen
set goals	gather information
decisive	open
organised	flexible

Readers who are familiar with Temperament and Psychological Type will appreciate that each individual personality type has a different order of dominance. Some functions come more naturally to some people and are preferred—while other functions which are least preferred and therefore unpractised will be hard work. Work on the unpractised functions may be considered as spiritual work. It is 'work', much the same as the grieving process is 'work'. If you know your personality type or have contemplated a self-selection process, the following table gives an example of functions in the order of preference:

ISTJ	ISFJ	INFJ	INTJ
Sensing	Sensing	Intuition	Intuition
Thinking	Feeling	Feeling	Thinking
Feeling	Thinking	Thinking	Feeling
Intuition	Intuition	Sensing	Sensing
ISTP	**ISFP**	**INFP**	**INTP**
Thinking	Feeling	Feeling	Thinking
Sensing	Sensing	Intuition	Intuition
Intuition	Intuition	Sensing	Sensing
Feeling	Thinking	Thinking	Feeling
ESTP	**ESFP**	**ENFP**	**ENTP**
Sensing	Sensing	Intuition	Intuition
Thinking	Feeling	Feeling	Thinking
Feeling	Thinking	Thinking	Feeling
Intuition	Intuition	Sensing	Sensing
ESTJ	**ESFJ**	**ENFJ**	**ENTJ**
Thinking	Feeling	Feeling	Thinking
Sensing	Sensing	Intuition	Intuition
Intuition	Intuition	Sensing	Sensing
Feeling	Thinking	Thinking	Feeling

The most dominant function is the most conscious function, while the least preferred function (Inferior function) is largely unconscious and this is where difficulties arise. An understanding of CG Jung's theory may help a person bring these feelings and experiences to the conscious mind where a rational exploration can take place. How to do this may be considered as 'soul work'. The MBTI is a first step in exploring one's preferred way of living in the world. The purpose of exploring a person's least preferred way of living in the world or considering a person's least developed preference, is to consider the coming together of opposites to make a more balanced whole. In this way the conscious and unconscious parts of our nature become joined and the degrees of our preferences become less extreme.

Inferior Function

- Seen when stressed, ill, tired or under the influence of drugs

- Behaviour can become compulsive—the person is unable to stop even if the conscious mind wants to. It can sabotage a person's conscious aims in life

- A tremendous charge of emotions is felt when the inferior function takes control

- Often ideas, thoughts and feelings that arise are not grounded in reality

- States of elation or hopelessness and gloom are experienced—moody

- Is the least preferred of your Four Functions—consequently the weakest and least developed and operates in your least important world

- For example, the Inferior Function of ENFJ is introverted thinking

- Each person has his/her strengths and weaknesses

- The behaviour of a person's Inferior Function causes the greatest suffering and stress

- Unless a high degree of awareness of one's potential weakness has been achieved, the Inferior Function remains primitive, childish and tyrannical.

MBTI Stress Guide

Personality Type	What nurtures them?	What may be a strain & stress?
Extroverts	Being given a chance to express and interact with the outer world—the opportunity to talk and share. Receiving cues from the environment.	Taking notes or writing reflectively in a journal. Having concentrated time for doing inner work.
Introverts	Being given a chance to write, reflect and meditate. Being given time to process ideas internally.	Having to give a spontaneous and off-the-cuff discussion or sharing of something personal. Having to make instant decisions.
Sensors	Having the specifics spelled out carefully and being included in a good experiential event which uses the five senses.	Being asked to imagine something that is unknown or 'airy-fairy'. Being expected to work with concepts.
Intuitives	Being given a chance to add to the situation with their own imagination and an opportunity to connect the learnings to their own experience.	Living 'in the moment' and doing detailed assignments such as creating schedules, proofreading or data entry.
Thinkers	Being given an opportunity to analyse a situation and to confront and challenge. Being required to give an objective opinion.	Experiencing powerlessness or lack of control. Being asked to accept a situation that is not based on logic or rational thinking.
Feelers	Receiving affirmations and positive rewards in a happy learning environment. They like to see the value of what is being learned for themselves and others.	Learning for the sake of the idea itself, with no other use or reward. Having to perform objective analysis and sticking to a conclusion, even if it is against their personal values.
Judgers	Having an agenda, a schedule, a plan or manual, handouts and charts. They like to finish on time—get the work done so that they can play.	Having no set agenda and just 'winging it'. Looking for random conversation to come up with a plan of action.
Perceivers	Having room to move, to know that there are rewards even if assignments are not completed. Enjoy an opportunity for self-pacing and self-determination.	Having to complete assignments on time without having the opportunity to change or explore ideas further.

   A SIMPLE GU IDE TO SELF - AWARENESS

Notes on Temperament

Throughout the ages, observers have repeatedly identified major patterns of behaviour. The ancient Sufis developed the Enneagram which describes patterns around a circle. Three of the positions on the circle are for people who are influenced by their heart, three positions are for people who are influenced by their head and three positions are for people who are influenced by their gut. The four central desires from Hindu wisdom—pleasure, success, duty and meaning are another example of human nature.

Twentieth century psychologists abandoned holistic observation of human behaviour for a microscopic examination of parts and traits. They saw all human beings as basically alike and the description of infinite differences replaced observation of the person as a whole. David Keirsey, a modern psychologist, noted themes in his various observations which sorted into four major patterns and he referred to these patterns as temperaments.

Keirsey believed that temperament was inborn, not acquired—just as Jung and Myers believed a person was born with a basic preference, for example, a dominant hand for writing. Temperament is present at birth and may be likened to the blueprint for an oak tree which is already in the seed. It differentiates, it doesn't change. By differentiating it becomes increasingly different from all else and more of what was present at birth. Jung called the process INDIVIDUATION.

There are four temperaments defined by Keirsey. Look for the following two letters from the four which describe your personality type:

SJ – These are the protectors or guardians. They have a natural disposition to observe and preserve. They are motivated by stability, security, and community. They are responsible, dutiful, structured, conservative, and naturally good at handling money. Life is a process of cultivating a comfortable life by organising and preserving their present environment. They are cautious of new situations. Their main strength is common sense and attention to detail.

SP – People with this temperament are the players. They value excitement and are incurable optimists who live to seize the moment. They are impatient with routine. To the SP life is a process of doing whatever feels good at the moment and seeking to make an impression at whatever they are doing. They relish danger, action, and new situations. Their main strength is that they find work as enjoyable as play and are flexible and not easily defeated.

NF – The idealist and pleaser with a natural ability to focus on possibilities for people and situations. They enjoy cultivating relationships, personal growth and generally making the world a better place. They are naturally altruistic and are willing to devote time and money to the betterment of others. They look for quality and will do without rather than settle for less. Their main strengths are their sense of mission for possibilities and natural empathy.

NT – The planner and visionary with a natural disposition to focus on future possibilities and concepts for systems and community. Life to these people is a process of acquiring expertise, relentlessly pursuing excellence and challenging conventional thought. They are motivated by ambition and achievement, preferring the new and improved rather than the tried and true. Their main strengths are intellectual ingenuity for problem solving and understanding systems.

Temperament can be fostered or stunted. It is the essence of team building. Self awareness/knowledge can assist a person to find the environment which best enhances their temperament.
For example:

NT	NF	SJ	SP
Stressors: Powerlessness Incompetence	**Stressors:** Insincerity Betrayal	**Stressors:** Abandonment Insubordination	**Stressors:** Constraint Clumsiness
When Stressed: Obsesses	**When Stressed:** Dissociates	**When Stressed:** Complains	**When Stressed:** Retaliates
What de-stresses? Reconfirmation of competence A new project	**What de-stresses?** Nurturing from self and others New quests	**What de-stresses?** Appreciation Inclusion in news and activities	**What de-stresses?** Shared experience Change Novelty
Motto: Be excellent in all things – promote efficiency	**Motto:** To thine own self be true – promote growth	**Motto:** Early to bed, early to rise – promote structure	**Motto:** Eat, drink and be merry – promote opportunity

IDEALIST
intuition & feeling NF

People with a temperament which combines intuition and feeling, are often referred to as IDEALISTS. They are interested in personal growth and improving the world. They are interested in becoming self-actualised and reaching their potential.

Questions asked

- How does this affect other's morale?
- Who needs to know?
- What impact does this have on the organisation's principles?
- What is most important to people?

They value:

- Autonomy and self determination
- Cooperation
- Harmony

Irritations at work

- Impersonal treatment
- Criticism
- Lack of positive feedback

GUARDIAN
sensing & judging SJ

People with a temperament which combines sensing and judging, are often referred to as GUARDIANS. They like to feel part of an organisation and have a place in the scheme of things. They are responsible and accountable and like to serve.

Questions asked

- What is the order?
- What is my duty?
- Why change?
- How is this justified?
- Does it work?

They value:

- Caution
- Carefulness
- Accuracy of work

Irritations at work

- Others not employing standard operating procedures
- Ignored deadlines
- Others not playing by the rules

RATIONAL
intuition & thinking NT

People with a temperament that combines intuition and thinking as opposed to intuition and feeling, are referred to as RATIONALS. They like to be competent and value knowledge and the power of the intellect. They are the visionaries and may seem to have their heads in the clouds and be sceptical.

Questions asked

- What is involved?
- What is the strategy?
- Who has the power?
- What is the system?

They value:

- Competence
- Intelligence
- Complexity
- Principles

Irritations at work

- Things that are redundant
- Stupid errors
- Illogical actions
- Impatient with human concerns

ARTISAN
sensing & perceiving SP

People with a temperament that combines sensing and perceiving as opposed to sensing and judging, enjoy action, freedom and spontaneity. They are the negotiators and make instantaneous decisions from many possibilities. They are difficult to tie down and are known as ARTISANS.

Questions asked

- What is the need right now?
- What are the stakes?
- Where is the crisis?
- How soon can we go and do?

They value:

- Flexibility
- Change
- Taking risks
- Action

Irritations at work

- Restrictions
- Being told how to work
- Doing it 'the way it's always been done'
- Not being able to give immediate response

IDEALIST
intuition & feeling NF

The NFs are the ones to sing praises of the good, the God in all of us, bringing the message of peace on earth and peace within ourselves.

For NFs, the magical moments of the Festive Season happen when people are speaking from the heart, revealing what it's like to be them, revealing the 'angels' inside them.

NFs don't need truckloads of intimacy, just a few moments of feeling really connected to someone, or delighted by someone. That's enough to make them feel that the Festive Season has lived up to its promise of being a special time.

The solid things for NFs are people's thoughts and feelings. An atmosphere that puts people at ease and lets them be themselves is going to feel more tangibly like a Festive Season than all the decorations in the world.

The NF message is that there is godliness in all of us, and the potential to save the world. That's why we should all be treated with mercy and seek peace and reconciliation with each other.

GUARDIAN
sensing & judging SJ

SJs are the ones who generally pull the big productions of the Festive season together and get everything ready on time.

SJs give parties and enjoy organising and providing a sense of control over the events.

SJs have a traditional get-together each year and remember and repeat customs.

SJs preserve tradition (not only at the Festive Season) and hold families together.

SJs adopt a group of people as family if no family is near.

Organising, repeating, remembering, insuring and securing keep SJs busy in the Festive Season. This behaviour is like a parent's responsibility and SJs seem to assume the parental role in all situations.

They like to prepare in advance and to be well organised ahead of time.

ARTISAN
sensing & perceiving SP

Be full of cheer, relax, and enjoy the Festive Season. Don't worry or work too hard. Don't be too serious. Have fun—that is what life is all about.

For SPs everything is last minute and full of action.

For SPs the stakes are high, but so is the glory.

They enjoy making things happen and can be quite daring and adventurous.

They like the outdoors to indoors.

They love to surprise people.

The SP likes to give gifts and so express feelings

in concrete ways.

VISIONARY
intuition & thinking NT

NTs have a need to innovate and set goals and these attributes extend to the Festive Season.

With their clever minds and deeper perspective they can make the Festive Season reach greater depths and widths.

NTs have a hard time in general with holidays and celebrations.

NTs have difficulty with repetition, details and 'things'.

NTs need to suspend their critical analytical thinking.

NTs feel useful if they can assist with design and concept.

The NT enjoys being competent and solving complex problems.

Confucius says: "Don't care about changing people, get behaviours right"

Caring always takes place within the context of a relationship
It requires compassion
The giving of unconditional love, i.e. positive energy...
Being oneself – being genuine...
Showing respect – prizing the person...
- Helen Parer

To care for others we must first care for ourselves. For example, we cannot dry a person with a towel that is already soaked. It just doesn't do the job. Caring for ourselves is not easy, for we have many 'selves' and wear many masks. A degree of self-awareness and realisation is essential for compassionate care. You may recognise yourself in the following:

The Real Self	This is the essential or spiritual you—the you that is totally unique and unlike any other person.
The Rational Self	This is the part that is in contact with reality, that estimates probabilities and risks and problem-solves.
The Emotional Self	Emotions are not always rational and may be part of suppressed life events and surface with conscious or unconscious triggers or projections.
The Observer Self	The observer is aware of our other selves and their actions and reactions and can influence change in behaviour.
The Critic	This part acts as judge, punisher and setter of standards. It may think that it has all the answers.
The Nurturer	This self is like a parent or figure head and seems to be on your side and cares for you.
The Not-OK Self	This self is rebellious, overly compliant in an effort to be lovable and worthy. It feels guilty and incomplete.

Once a person has some understanding of their personality type, they can more carefully own and respect the strengths they possess. Once a person has had knowledge of their strengths and preferences they can be more aware of the neglected parts of their personality. Because a person's introversion, sensing and thinking may all be poorly developed, they may find themselves defensive and sensitive about these areas of their personality. As a consequence, they project their poorly developed attitude and functions upon someone who represents strength in the areas of their weakness. Needlessly harmful feelings of criticism and dislike may arise towards that person because the least developed parts of our personality are seen in another person. Jung (1985 p.592) writes:

> *As nobody can become aware of his individuality unless he is closely and responsibly related to his fellow beings, he is not withdrawing to an egoistic desert when he tries to find himself. He can only discover himself when he is deeply and unconditionally related to some, and generally related to a great many, individuals with whom he has a chance to compare and from who he is able to discriminate himself.*

Jung says that the first part of a person's life is taken up with ego activities—playing the game of life, developing the tools for survival in the various aspects of life. He says that the second part of a person's life is taken up with commentary about the game, when a person tries to make sense of the 'game' of life and find meaning. To have a knowledgeable person assisting in the commentary and explaining the rules, successes, and failures, is helpful. This guide may be a religious leader, an inner guide (for example, dreams, meditation, inner journeys), inspired writings, as well as the people who nurses and carers meet in their daily work. Those we seek to serve can be wonderful teachers.

Journey Through Life

The images associated with 'journey' are ones of preparation (such as gaining an education to equip one for a comfortable travel period), the highs and lows of the journey itself (such as loves and relationships, gains and losses and health and ill health) and the arrival or terminus, when the soul travelling on spirit or energy particles separates from the physical body and joins an unseen world. The word 'journey' reminds a person of change, great testing, and the process of becoming. Jung called the journey of the development of the psyche or soul the process of individuation.

For nurses and carers who support people at the end of their life (due to disease or age) it is important to have an appreciation of the significance and the role of soul in the final days or weeks of life. As the work of soul is largely unconscious, nurses and carers need to have skills in gaining access to what is held in the unconscious. Mythology, fairy stories, universal gods and goddesses all help a person recognise parts of themselves that are not conscious. A helpful exercise is to plot one's journey through life on steppingstones across a river. Each stone will be a reminder of times in a person's life that were secure, slippery or even scary. There will be the memory of feelings as one stone was left for another. Life review is an important part of the end of life process. It may be too painful for the person who is dying but can often be successfully facilitated by encouraging stories from friends and relatives. The journey is a personal story of responses to the challenges of life—it is a work in progress— of becoming.

> *It is more important to know what sort of person has the disease than to know what sort of disease a person has.*
> *- Hippocrates 500BC*
>
> *Life has meaning when we give ourselves meaning.*
> *- Margaret Cain - Dominican Sister and Clinical Psychologist*
>
> *We must learn to draw on our inner resources, to define ourselves in terms of the feedback we receive from our own internal valuing system rather than trying to fit ourselves into some ill-fitting stereotyped role.*
> *- Elisabeth Kubler-Ross (1975, p 164)*

Exploring C G Jung's Theories

The purpose for exploring Jung's theories is to bring some understanding to the deeper spiritual issues that are frequently faced in the final phase of life in those people receiving supportive care. By being aware of our personal strivings towards individuation, it is easier to have empathy with another person as well as receive richer personal lives for ourselves. Healing the psyche or soul is invisible work. It involves an exploration of the unconscious parts of the Self. Larry Dossey (1993), physician and author who has published widely honouring the power of prayer and mind/body connection, says that one of the practically unchallenged facts of modern psychology is that we live the vast bulk of our psychic lives in the unconscious. He says that the unconscious needs to be explored, for it is wiser than we are and is our interface with God.

Individuation

The process of becoming whole. The process of becoming what we are, of being true to our innate selves. Finding our unique way. The path to the centre of being. It is a process.

Consciousness

That part of ourselves of which we are aware. *"Our consciousness does not create itself—it wells up from unknown depths."* Whitmont (1991 p 50)

Unconscious

The part of ourselves of which we are NOT aware. It is made up of two parts: the personal unconscious and the collective unconscious. It is limited by perceptions of the senses. Jung (1985 p 419) referred to the unconscious as possessing better sources of information than the conscious mind—which has only sense perceptions available to it. He defines the unconscious as: Everything of which I know, but of which I am not at the moment thinking; everything of which I was once conscious but have now forgotten; everything perceived by my senses, but not noted by my conscious mind; everything which, involuntarily and without paying attention to it, I feel, think, remember, want, and do; all the future things that are taking shape in me and will sometime come to consciousness: all this is the content of the unconscious.

> *Everything of which I know, but of which I am not at the moment thinking; everything of which I was once conscious but have now forgotten; everything perceived by my senses, but not noted by my conscious mind; everything which, involuntarily and without paying attention to it, I feel, think, remember, want, and do; all the future things that are taking shape in me and will sometime come to consciousness: all this is the content of the unconscious.*

Collective Unconscious and Archetypes

The collective unconscious is those parts of ourselves of which we are NOT aware that are common to all people.

Archetype

> *… a dimension of consciousness that contains all of us collectively and yet somehow also individually. For although the way you express your archetypes is unique to you, these energies correspond to the archetypes of other people in your life. They interact. Everyone has a Child archetype, for example, and so the inner Child in you connects you to the inner Child within everyone else.*
>
> *- Myss (2001, p 8)*

Examples of archetypes:

The wise old man or woman, the good mother, the saboteur, the victim, the wounded child, the queen, the teacher, the warrior, the artist, the actor, the prostitute (selling values and ideals for the sake of security or comfort, as well as sex).

The following may be thought of as archetypes:

Self – The centre of the person. The central guidance system. The centre and content of the total personality—including the God within.

Persona – An archetype of adaptation to the outer world. It often contains the collective ideals of the surrounding social environment or 'tribe'. The 'persona' is the organised image of 'self' formed to present to the outside world—partly conscious and partly unconscious. John Welch (1982) writes that in the early part of life the persona (or mask) needs to have a healthy identity and have roots in the outer world to form a firm base for exploring the inner world.

Shadow – The shadow is unconscious and is made up of the personal characteristics and potentialities of which the individual is unaware or does not wish to own. Often it contains parts of us which are not compatible with the persona's image of ourselves—traits that we are not only trying to hide from others but also from ourselves. It contains unlived lives which may be seen as uncharacteristic behaviour—for example, the responsible family man who falls in love with a younger woman. It may contribute to 'terminal restlessness', as what has been held in the unconscious rises without the restraints of ego ideals. Singh (1999 pp 71–72) writes that the first transformative experience of healing and integration is the joining of the Persona and the Shadow. A person needs to own all of their parts:

> *All of the parts we have consistently disowned throughout our lives up until this point have been projected onto 'external' reality and have been loaded with affect and value judgements.*

The shadow is connected to the Inferior Function (a person's least preferred way of being in the world).

Anima – The unconscious feminine, usually thought of as being in the male. It gives relationship and relatedness to a man's consciousness. If not integrated into consciousness, a man may be without animation, abstract and swept by moods. Unconscious qualities may be projected onto another person and prevent a person from being objective and relating authentically.

Animus – The unconscious masculine, usually thought of as being in the female. It gives the capacity for reflection, deliberation and the ability to find meaning in ideas. If not integrated into consciousness, a woman may become very opinionated and unable to focus clearly. As with the anima, unconscious qualities may be projected onto another person and prevent a person from being objective and relating authentically.

The following diagram shows the parts of the Self.

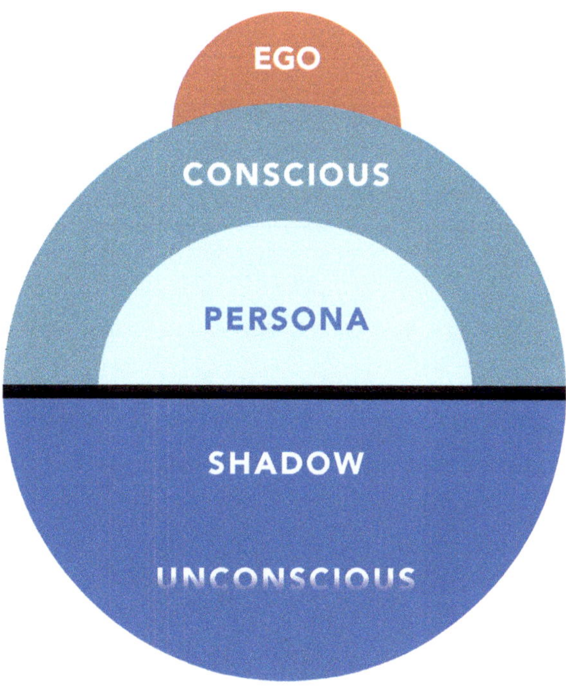

The following diagram shows the collective unconscious and how it is joined to the personal unconscious. This is the realm of the archetype and also the 'pool of ideas' as described by Plato.

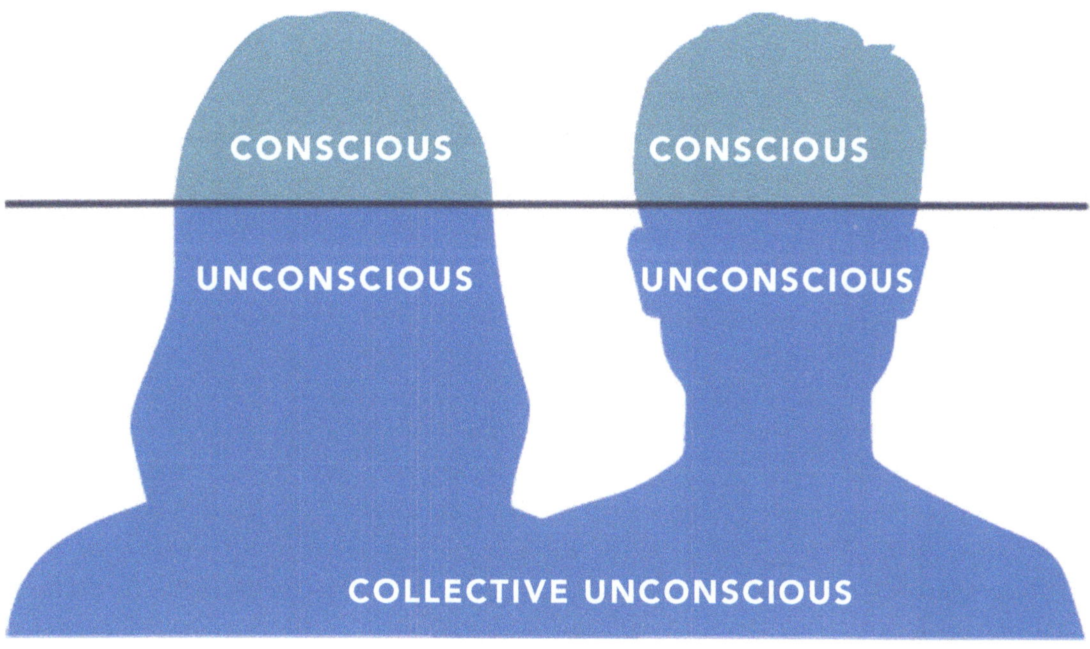

Ego

The first half of life is spent in developing an ego, which we must then unlearn in the second part of life. This is a paradox as so much of spirituality is. Wapnick (1987) writes that true spiritual maturity is not possible until we come of age. He says that many of the relationships in the first part of our lives are the building blocks through which we will later learn the lessons of forgiveness that will lead us back to spiritual connectedness. Consider the following points:

- Ego is the sum of the differences which separate each human person from others

- Ego is a lens through which a person views life—ideas, feelings, memories and perceptions (may be distorted)

- One theory is that a survival gene (a compulsion to live) is to be found in ego.
  Singh (1999 p 199) writing on spiritual transformation at the time of death says:

  > *Evolving consciousness is still assaulted by the death throes of the ego's will to live. The self passes mercilessly, again and again, through the purgative processes of the transformative fields—Experience, Empty Mind, and Wisdom. Although enlarging, the process entails deep suffering.*

- Growth and consciousness is achieved when ego-self dies to the deeper meaning of death.

  > *The old structures of ego identity are seen to have no reality whatsoever, can no more be held onto than can a billow of smoke.*
  > *- Singh (1999 p 199)*

- The conscious and personal unconscious Self join the collective unconscious—the universal stream of consciousness.

This means no more clinging to a sense of identity or 'Me-ness" and wanting more of those things which strengthen the ego—money, power, time. Rather it is a time of 'letting go' or surrender to the larger picture of life. Calabria and Macrae (1994 p 145) record that Florence Nightingale called this world a reflection of a greater reality and she wrote the following as a twenty-six year old woman:

> *I cannot pretend to speak of death as a misfortune… Death is the arch of triumph under which the soul passes to live again in a purer and freer atmosphere.*

Changing 'Me-ness' is threatening. In many cultures rites of passage and rituals assist a person through change. For example, there are religious rituals such as baptism, confirmation, marriage; there are rituals for leaving school, reaching 21 years of age and graduation and retirement ceremonies; there are the rituals around birth and death, the harvest festivals and thanksgiving rituals which celebrate the changing seasons. There are the rituals of hospitality and rituals practised by the medical and nursing professions.

On life after death

Janet Macrae (1994 p 146) shares Florence Nightingale's belief on life after death:

> For Nightingale the question of death was relatively simple: as each individual embodies unique qualities that cannot be duplicated, it would not be consistent with God's benevolent nature to obliterate that being. Because it is God's plan to raise mankind from imperfection to perfection, death must initiate a different mode of existence, one that allows for continued development.

Jung (1985 p 347) says:

> ...we are dependent for our myth of life after death upon the meagre hints of dreams and spontaneous revelations from the unconscious... They can, however, serve as suitable bases for mythic amplification; they give the probing intellect the raw material which is indispensable for its vitality.

Jung (1985 p 349) says that he can well imagine that he might have lived in former centuries and encountered questions there that he was not yet able to answer, and that he had to be born again because he had not fulfilled the task that had been given to him. Writing about life after death these are his thoughts:

> When I die, my deeds will follow along with me—that is how I imagine it. I will bring with me what I have done. In the meantime it is important to ensure that I do not stand at the end with empty hands.

Writing about the many paradoxes in life, Dossey (1992 p 211) notes that many spiritually aware people view health and adversity as, somehow, being required in their lives. He quotes Jung's theory that the psyche is a balancing act between the conscious and the unconscious parts of a person and while the conscious part of the person prefers health, the unconscious realises that life is not so simple and that adversity and illness are necessary. This is reflected in many traditional populations where disease is in fact viewed as disease—the physical condition is the symptom of a deeper spiritual problem.

What does this have to do with life after death? Elisabeth Kubler-Ross (1975) says that death is the final stage of growth in this life. There is no total death, for only the body dies. The self or spirit, or whatever you may wish to label it, is eternal. I have found that in my life the MBTI and Jung's theories have been a valuable first step in my creative self-development.

Warrior

The warrior's approach is to say 'yes' to life:
'yes' to it all.
Participate joyfully in the sorrows of the world.

We cannot cure the world of sorrows,
but we can choose to live in joy.
When we talk about settling the
world's problems,
we're barking up the wrong tree.

The world is perfect. It's a mess.
It has always been a mess.
We are not going to change it.
Our job is to straighten out
our own lives.

- Joseph Campbell

Bibliography

Briggs-Myers, I. & Myers, P.B. (1995). Gifts differing: Understanding personality type. Palo Alto, California: Davies-Black Publishing

Briggs Myers, I., McCaulley, M.H., Quenk, N.L. and Hammer, A.L. (1998) MBTI® Manual A Guide to the Development and Use of the Myers-Briggs Type Indicator®, Third Edition

Bates, Marilyn & Keirsey, David W. Please Understand Me. Del Mar, CA: Prometheus Nemesis

Hirsh, Sandra Krebs, Introduction to Type and Teams. Palo Alto, CA: Consulting Psychologists Press

Jeffries, William C (1991), True to Type. Hampton Roads Publishing Co., Charlottesville, VA

Jung, Carl G. (1969) Man and His Symbols. Garden City, N.Y.: Doubleday.

Peck, M. Scott. (1997). In heaven as on earth: A vision of the Afterlife. Glasgow, GB: Caledonian International Book Manufacturing.

Bates, M and Keirsey, DW (1978) Please Understand Me. Del Mar, CA: Prometheus Nemesis Books.

Campbell, J (1971) The Portable Jung. New York: Viking Press.

Campbell, J (1973) The Hero With A Thousand Faces. Princeton, NJ: Princeton University Press.

Calabria, MD and Macrae, JA (1994) Suggestions for Thought by Florence Nightingale. Philadelphia: University of Pennsylvania.

Dossey, L (1991) Meaning and Medicine. New York: Bantam Books.

Dossey, L (1993) Healing words: The power of prayer and practice of medicine. New York: Harper-Collins Francisco.

Johnson, RA (1991) Owning Your Own Shadow: Understanding the Dark Side of the Psyche. New York: Harper & Rowe

Jung CG (1985) Memories, Dreams and Reflections. UK: Flamingo.

Kubler-Ross, E (1975) Death—the final stage of growth. New York: Simon & Schuster, Inc.

Maslow, A (1968) Toward a Psychology of Being. 2nd edition Princeton: Von Nostrand.

Myers Briggs, I and McCaulley, M H (1985) A Guide to the Development and Use of the Myers-Briggs Type Indicator. Consulting Psychologists Press: Palo Alto USA.

Briggs-Myers, I. & Myers, P. B. (1995). Gifts differing: Understanding personality type. Palo Alto, California: Davies-Black Publishing.

Myss, C (2001) Sacred Contracts. Aust. & NZ: Bantam.

Oliver P (2005) A Passion For Caring, Book 4 A Six Part Holistic Learning Series in Palliative Care and Gerontology. Adelaide: NurseLink Australia Pty Ltd.

Palmer, H (1988) The Enneagram: The Definitive Guide to the Ancient System for Understanding Yourself and the Others in Your Life. New York, NY; Harper & Row, Publishers, Singh, KD (1999) The Grace in Dying. Dublin: Gill & Macmillan Ltd.

Wagner, J (1996) Enneagram Spectrum of Personality Styles: An Introductory Guide. Portland, Oregon: Metamorphous Press.

Wapnick, K (1987) The Meaning of Forgiveness. London: Arkana Paperbacks.

Welch, J (1982) Spiritual pilgrims: Carl Jung and Teresa of Avila. New York: Paulist Press.

Whitmont, ED (revised 1991) The Symbolic Quest, Basic Concepts of Analytical Psychology. Princeton, New Jersey: Princeton University Press.